I Have Awesome is an uplifting and encouraging story depicting a family's outcome that depends on their community, each other, and, most importantly, God—the same God who made Becky, Jon, Jacob, and Hannah in His image, with a plan and purpose for each of them.

The reader of *I Have Awesome* will be inspired by the lessons in this book–not to give up in tough circumstances but to seek help from others and the Lord, who never leaves or forsakes.

Greg McDougall,
Director of special needs ministry, twenty-five years.
Woodside Bible Church

The Richey's perspective on life is truly inspirational. The writing is enjoyable and easy to understand, making it accessible for all readers. What stands out the most to me is the fact that there is a takeaway for everyone who reads this book.

Elanor Constable,
M. Ed., Special Education
Autism Endorsement

Jon and Becky Richey embody a life freely offered in humble faith to the Lord. When God gave them two autistic children to raise, there were choices they had to make about how they would live their lives, both professionally and personally. They chose the very narrow road of faith, choosing to count as blessing a life that many would see as curse. Now many years later, they are an exemplar to all of us of what a life laid down in faith looks like. Their children are joyful Christians, filled with love and affection for one another, their parents, and the people around them. To be with them and see the way they seamlessly care for one another in sacrificial ways . . . now decades into the rhythms of a life shaped by the Gospel . . . is like a master class in a life well lived.

The Rev Lou Bayly Mahr, Deacon
Church of the Resurrection
Washington, DC

What a pleasure and privilege it is to highly endorse "I Have Awesome ".

I was taken on an emotional and inspiring journey while reading this honest and vulnerable book of family love. Each chapter opened up a window into a family's life whose faith, laughter, and resilience made me so proud to call them friends and friends of the farm!

Knowing the Richey family has enriched my life in so many ways. As the founder and director of the Clarkston Family Farm I have personally been the recipient of their unique and meaningful contributions. Jacob and Hannah have both contributed in many impactful ways throughout the years and Jacob, in particular, has become an essential part of our Barnyard Buddy Farm Team. Even with everything they hold each day, they continue to find the strength, time, and energy to give back to their community! This book is a wonderful example of their generosity to that wider community as they share their triumphs and struggles, as well as the intense grief and awakening to a new life, a different life certainly than they imagined, but a life that is indeed AWESOME.

"We can do hard things" is a saying in my family, and it has helped us get through difficult and seemingly impossible times, but in reading, and re-reading this book, I realize that doing the hard things is just the first step. The "celebrating the hard things" and accepting that all of it is God's will, allows for the rainbows in the rain. A letting go of the life you thought you would live, and embracing the life that is meant for you to live, makes all the difference. Life is a beautiful disaster sometimes and sometimes it's just beautiful. The Richey Family embodies and illustrates everything that is hard, and complicated and funny and, yes, beautiful and their book is a must read. I promise it will make you laugh and cry and love, even more, our endless spectrum of possibilities.

Chelsea O'Brien, Founder and Executive Director
Clarkston Family Farm- a non-profit educational farm for kids of all ages and abilities

I HAVE AWESOME (AUTISM)

FINDING JOY ON OUR JOURNEY

JON AND BECKY RICHEY

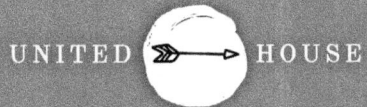

I Have Awesome (Autism) —Copyright ©2025 by Jon and Becky Richey
Published by UNITED HOUSE Publishing

All rights reserved. No portion of this book may be reproduced or shared in any form–electronic, printed, photocopied, recording, or by any information storage and retrieval system, without prior written permission from the publisher. The use of short quotations is permitted.

Scriptures taken from the Holy Bible, New International Version®, NIV®. Copyright © 1973, 1978, 1984, 2011 by Biblica, Inc.™ Used by permission of Zondervan. All rights reserved worldwide. www.zondervan.com The "NIV" and "New International Version" are trademarks registered in the United States Patent and Trademark Office by Biblica, Inc.™

ISBN: 978-1-952840-62-3

UNITED HOUSE Publishing
Waterford, Michigan
info@unitedhousepublishing.com
www.unitedhousepublishing.com

Photography:
Family Photos

Cover Layout and Interior Design:
Matt Russell, In The Light Creative, matt@inthelightcreative.com

Printed in the United States of America
2025—First Edition

SPECIAL SALES
Most UNITED HOUSE books are available at special quantity discounts when purchased in bulk by corporations, organizations, and special-interest groups. For information, please e-mail orders@unitedhousepublishing.com

We dedicate this book to Hannah and Jacob. You inspire us daily. Thank you for all you have taught us about faith, joy, and life! We love you more than you can imagine.

Table of Contents

Foreword 11

Prologue 13

ONE **This is Us** 17

TWO **A Mother's Intuition** 21

THREE **The Diagnoses** 25

FOUR **Holland** 33

FIVE **Building Blocks** 41

SIX **Finding Their Niche** 61

SEVEN **Lessons Learned and Still Learning** 69

EIGHT **Grace Upon Grace** 79

Epilogue 87

Acknowledgements 89

Notes 91

About the Author 93

Foreword

I have had the privilege of knowing Jon and Becky Richey, the authors of this book, for over twenty years. Our paths first crossed when their children, Hannah and Jacob, were in elementary school, during my time as a speech pathologist and coordinator of the Autism Spectrum Disorders Program. Later, as Executive Director of Special Education, I had numerous opportunities to work closely with both parents, and I witnessed firsthand the strong advocacy, intuition, and resilience that guided them through every step of their children's educational journey.

Over the course of my career, I've collaborated with countless parents. While everyone's path is unique, Jon and Becky stand out for their extraordinary ability to see and nurture the individual gifts of their children, rather than focusing on expectations imposed by outside forces. Even in challenging moments, they embraced optimism and celebrated each milestone, big or small, with genuine joy and enthusiasm.

In this book, Jon and Becky share the story of raising two children with autism into adulthood, offering a candid heartfelt account of both the trials and triumphs that shaped their family. Their openness and vulnerability shine through on every page. By inviting us into their world, this remarkable couple offers hope and encouragement to families on a similar path. This book is a powerful testament to the strength of a parent's love and a reminder that with faith and unwavering acceptance, we can reveal the unique gifts in every child.

Kathy Christopher, M.S., CCC-SLP
Executive Director of Special Education (retired)

Prologue

It was July 1994; we moved to Denver, Colorado. Becky and I were newlyweds from Michigan. Because we are both very social, we quickly met a group of young married couples at our church. One of the guys in our group, John, invited some men to go hiking in the Rocky Mountains. Though he invited all of the men in the group, only three of us accepted the invitation. We wondered why the others had declined and even laughed when he said it would only be the four of us. Why were the guys from Texas, Oregon, and Michigan the only ones excited about this adventure?

On the day of the hike, I was filled with anticipation. When we arrived at the trailhead, John wrote our names on a notepad inside a wooden box. I asked him what he was doing, and he explained he was recording our names so the rangers could contact our families if we went missing.

We began hiking up some small hills, and immediately, I felt winded. Why? Well, the highest point in Michigan is 1,980 feet. The lowest point in our new home of Colorado was over 3,000 feet. So, even in Denver, a short walk could make you feel out of breath. We kept hiking, and I felt increasingly tired, wondering if I would make it.

After hiking just a few miles, we found a fork in the trail. John shared with the three inexperienced hikers that we had a choice. Both trails would get us to our intended destination. One was eight miles long, and the other was seven miles long. John said, "There is a reason the trail on the left is a mile shorter. It is more difficult, but the view is amazing." Of course, we three amateurs wanted an amazing Rocky Mountain view, so we went with the seven-mile trail.

We hiked into a valley. It had a majestic view of the Red Buffalo Pass. It was bigger than anything I had ever seen! I was overwhelmed by the beauty of this enormous mountain pass and wondered how many hikers had hiked to the top and lived to talk about it. I remember thinking, *Surely this is the beautiful view they told us about. This is where we stop, eat our lunch, turn around, and go back.* I asked John where we were eating lunch, and he pointed to the top of the Red Buffalo Pass. I reminded him the three of us were inexperienced hikers. He said, "Jon, by the time we are done, you will be an expert hiker!"

As we hiked up the pass, my legs were burning. I was falling behind the others and struggling with each step. Zippy, John's friend and one of the four in the group, was making it look easy. He was way ahead of everyone (hence the name "Zippy"). He saw me struggling and headed down the trail to meet me. He gave me some pointers and words of encouragement, which I found very helpful. Then Zippy began to ask questions about me, Becky, and what brought us to Denver. Suddenly, we were at our lunch spot—the top of the Red Buffalo Pass. It would be an understatement to say the view was spectacular. It brought immediate tears to my eyes. I was so overwhelmed by the beauty of God's creation. We could see mountain range after mountain range. There was a beautiful, small lake in the valley on the other side of the pass with water so clear you could see trout swimming in it, even from a thousand feet above. I told Zippy, "Had I known this hike would be so tough, I wouldn't have come. But now that I am here, at the top, I am so glad I did." I will never forget Zippy's response. He said, "God is like that with us. If we knew what lay ahead, we would likely give up. But then God's grace helps us see His beauty and purposes in the difficulties in our lives."

On the top of that beautiful mountain, the words of Jeremiah 29:11 came to me: "'For I know the plans I have for you,' declares the Lord. 'Plans to prosper you, and not to harm you, to give you a hope and a future.'" The prophet Jeremiah was speaking to people who were in Babylonian captivity. God was telling them, "I got this! Trust me, and know you will be fine. In fact, you will prosper!"

For all of us, there are unexpected circumstances in our lives. We do not plan for them, but they happen. Some are easier to manage, while others are longer, even lifelong. It may be a job loss, terminal illness, broken relationships, or even a lifelong disability. These things can be overwhelming and make us feel unable to continue in our own strength. Truth be told, we cannot do it alone.

Becky and I are on a journey we did not choose. In fact, in all honesty, had God told us we would raise two children with Autism, we may have responded with the same words our son, Jacob, often uses: "You're teasing!" But now that we are on this journey, we would never trade it. Like the 17-mile hike back in 1994, there have been some steep climbs, strenuous paths, and lots of unknowns. Yet, it has been breathtakingly amazing, spectacular, and beautiful.

We hope that writing this book about our journey with Hannah and Jacob will encourage many. It is not an easy journey, but it is worth the climb. Thank you for allowing us to share our story. Now come, let's take a journey!

ONE

This Is Us

Our story began with a whirlwind romance spanning our first date to our wedding day just nine months later. And our wedding day—what a beginning to our life adventure! Who chooses to get married in Iowa in January? The day held horrific blizzards with wind chills at negative 50 degrees. The stomach flu tore in with a vengeance on our big day. The most severely affected and sickest were the father of the bride, the groom, and the best man. And when we say sick, we mean sick! Becky's dad missed the entire reception. Jon took a nap between the pictures and the wedding. The groomsmen woke him and said, "Hey Jon, it's time to get married!" Mark, our best man, had a chair brought to him during the ceremony so he could sit down and not pass out. We even placed trash cans in the front row if anyone needed to vomit. Yep, it was that bad. During our vows, the line "in sickness and in health" brought lots of laughter throughout the church. Little did we know those vows would be tested much further in years to come. The song *Find Us Faithful* was sung at our wedding and was our prayer for our life together—that we would always be faithful to God's calling and direction.

During our first few years of marriage, Jon was a youth pastor in Spring Lake, Michigan. We were neck-deep in teenagers. We loved doing ministry together and pouring into the lives of students and their families. Then, we realized Jon needed more training, so we went to Denver Seminary. We loaded everything and took off like the Beverly Hillbillies. We did not have jobs lined up, but we knew God called us to go, and He would provide for us.

Shortly after we arrived, Becky started working full-time as a nurse at Denver Children's Hospital on the oncology/bone marrow transplant unit. It was a challenging job, but she loved it. Jon started taking courses full-time and worked a few different jobs throughout our two years in Denver. God blessed us with an amazing church and group of friends. Times were very tough financially. We were committed to "no student loan debt." We knew we wanted to start our family soon, and our prayer was for Becky to stay home with our kids. People jokingly referred to the seminary as "The Fertile Crescent." Between that and our young married group at church, we were surrounded by pregnancies and babies. Soon, it would be our turn, or so we thought.

Then began our journey of infertility. Unless you have endured this struggle, you just cannot comprehend the level of pain and grief involved. So many of our friends were starting their families, and it seemed they had no struggle. It was a lonely and isolated time. Innocent comments became daggers through our grieving hearts. We quit attending our young married class for a while because it was too emotionally taxing.

Thankfully, our struggle with infertility lasted only a little over a year. We began seeing an infertility specialist. To our surprise, Becky became pregnant with Hannah the very next month. We chose 1 Samuel 1:27-28 as our verses for our baby: "I prayed for this child and the LORD has granted me what I asked of Him. So now, I give him to the LORD. For his whole life, he will be given to the LORD." This beautiful prayer by Hannah in the Bible inspired our daughter's name.

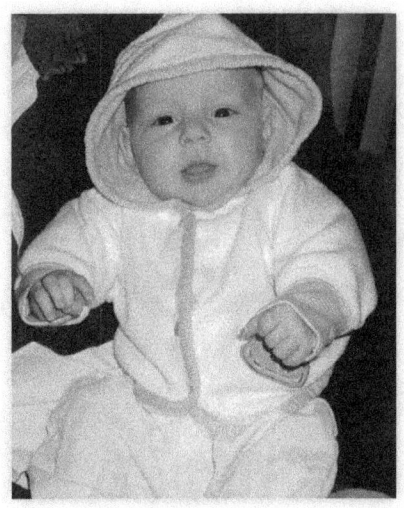

Several weeks later, Jon graduated from Denver Seminary, and we were off to Tracy, California. Jon was offered a youth pastor position at a church there. We were the Beverly Hillbillies again, 2.0.

Shortly after Hannah's first birthday, we were surprised and elated to find Becky was pregnant with Jacob. She made Jon buy a second pregnancy test to confirm because we could not believe it was positive. On our first visit with Becky's doctor, he said, "Well, whatever the problem was, you're cured!" We were living the dream. Life was great.

TWO

A Mother's Intuition

Hannah met all her developmental milestones, including beginning to put words together at fifteen months old. Then, suddenly, it was as if she flipped a switch. She began to withdraw into her own little world. It felt like we were losing our ability to reach her. She also started having some significant behaviors, including hour-long tantrums. Becky continued to reach out to her pediatrician, his only response being, "Are you reading to her? Are you spending time with her?" Obviously, that was less than helpful and extremely hurtful. Month after month, we felt like we were losing more and more of our baby, and no one would listen or help.

To be honest, autism was not on our radar; the Autism world was different then. We did not know a single family who had a child with autism. This was the very beginning of the internet age. We did not have a PC, access to the internet, or any resources. Our only exposure to autism was the movie *Rain Man*. We did not know how to proceed. It was a very isolated time for Becky and Hannah. "Mommy and me" things just didn't work. We tried to provide play dates, but Hannah often ended up alone in her room. Of course, we also began questioning our parenting as we felt as if we were doing something wrong. We were first-time parents and in over our heads. And then, of course, there were the looks. The judgment. The gossip. We needed help. We knew what they were thinking. We had thought things like that ourselves about other people's kids, and now, here we were.

One specific experience still haunts us all these years later. We were at our local McDonald's, sitting in the play area. It was time to leave, and Hannah was definitely not in agreement. She had a full-blown meltdown. Jon ended up carrying her to the car, kicking and screaming, but before we could make our exit, we were "blessed" with many condescending looks, stares, and comments. We overheard one customer say, "Give me that kid for a day; I'll straighten her out." We were so defeated and embarrassed, but more than anything, we simply didn't know what to do.

Becky talked with the pediatrician and anyone who would listen, looking for answers. They told us not to worry. Kids develop at different rates. She was fine. But inside, we knew it was not fine. Hannah's behaviors and tantrums were escalating, often to the point where we were afraid to take her out in public. We felt overwhelmed and scared, and we had another baby on the way. How were we going to manage this with a newborn?

We chose to keep the gender of our babies a surprise until they were born. We were thrilled when Jacob was born. We were blessed with two beautiful children: one girl and one boy! Jacob was such a good baby, so easy-going and relaxed. Our friend commented, "If you didn't know he was here, you could easily forget about him." Yet, despite this, Hannah's behaviors continued to escalate.

A Mother's Intuition

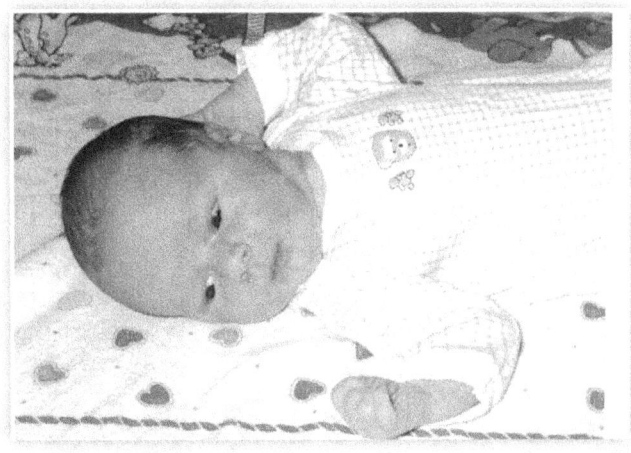

During the following year, we began to feel more isolated and overwhelmed. Taking the kids out anywhere was almost impossible, especially for Becky alone. It was exhausting and almost always embarrassing.

A few months before Hannah's third birthday, Becky finally talked with a different pediatrician. He asked her to complete a simple two-page screening that included just 16 "yes" or "no" questions. That was enough to get us a referral finally. This was the first mention of the "A" word . . . Autism. No, it can't be! Not our baby. She's okay. She's just strong-willed and stubborn. After all, she is a redhead! The more we tried to engage her in play, books, or anything, the more she seemed to pull away. We were losing our baby!

THREE

The Diagnoses

Our world was about to be rocked. December of 1999 through May of 2002 was filled with several life-altering diagnoses for our family. We had no idea what lay ahead.

Once our doctor made the referral for Hannah, the regional center responded quickly with in-home evaluations. From there, they scheduled an in-office multi-disciplinary team evaluation. We were so thankful for Valley Mountain Regional Center and for all the support they provided. On the day of Hannah's evaluation, they provided a parent support person. We were anxious about the evaluation because we just wanted some answers. While we waited, Becky conversed with the support person, and she said something we remember to this day: "Whatever happens in there today, remember, she's still your same little girl, the same as when she went in." That was just what we needed to hear.

That day, December 6, 1999, our Hannah received her Autism diagnosis—a "life-altering disability," per the team. We cannot explain how we felt that day; we do not even remember. We just kept reminding each other God is good. Our heads were spinning. We were overwhelmed, confused, relieved,

I HAVE AWESOME (AUTISM)

sad, and ready to get to work. We were willing to do whatever was needed to be done to support our girl. Later that day, a whole new way of life began. We were entering our new normal. We made many phone calls to seek out the best "therapy" and ways to educate ourselves. What would this do to our family, our marriage, and what about Jacob? How will we be able to give him all he needs? Our life was anything but typical, which is what we longed for—just a bit of normalcy.

To complicate things further, we were in the process of selling our home and moving back to the Midwest. We knew we needed to be closer to family for support with our kids. It was a difficult decision. We were beyond sad to say goodbye to many beautiful friends in California.

A couple of months after we moved to Mitchell, South Dakota, we began to have concerns about Jacob and his development. He only used a few words, did not play appropriately with his toys, and had poor eye contact. We could not even entertain the thought of another Autism diagnosis. We kept trying to convince ourselves everything was okay, but inside, we were wrestling with this and feeling so alone. Oh Lord, please, not both of our babies!

The Diagnoses

That spring, Jacob had tubes placed in his ears due to chronic ear infections. *Surely, this was an explanation!* We thought. Try as we might, we could not shake the feeling we knew all too well. After the surgery, we saw very little improvement in his language development. Next, the doctors ordered a hearing evaluation. When the test came back normal, Becky broke into tears. The technician was confused. We explained that, in our eyes, a slight hearing deficit would be welcomed news compared to the diagnosis we were dreading, but, in our hearts, knew it was coming.

The early intervention team started evaluations. Throughout the summer, they worked with Jacob once a week. We tried to work with him as often as we could at home, feeling the need to be "therapeutic" all the time. We simply longed to enjoy our boy and not evaluate and critique everything he did and did not do. Very little progress was made. In September, he turned two. His symptoms escalated. We felt like we could not reach him. Jacob began more intensive one-on-one therapy. We were juggling both kids' therapy schedules, but we did it, desperate for anything to help. That was the worst part, the helplessness. We bargained with God, asking, "Why? Isn't one enough? Why both of our babies? Who will watch out for them when we are gone? What will their futures hold?" This is where trusting in God and his goodness became essential. Our lifeline. Our only hope.

On December 6, 2000, exactly one year to the day after Hannah's diagnosis, Jacob received his Autism Diagnosis. We were incredibly overwhelmed but pressed on because we had no choice. Our kids needed us. We did it for them. At this time, our marriage took a back seat. We were struggling and in survival mode. Sadly, this is not an uncommon occurrence for special needs families. We are thankful for God's grace and goodness in helping us to sustain our marriage. We continue to work diligently to make the health of our marriage a priority. To this day, we strive to incorporate consistent date nights into our schedule, which can be very difficult when you still need to find a "babysitter" for your 6'5" manchild with facial hair.

Our at-home stress spilled over into Jon's work life, making it almost impossible for him to focus on his job and ministry. Short of a few friends, we felt very alone and unsupported in that setting. It was time for a career change. He began working at an in-patient treatment facility for troubled teenage girls. Becky also returned to work part-time, working the night shift at a nursing home.

We were trying to hold it together and make it day-to-day most of the time. To be honest, it was chaotic. We were stretched so thin. So many feelings and emotions consumed us. We were exhausted. The kids were on opposite sleep schedules for several years, with Jacob often waking before Hannah fell asleep. Jon slept in front of Jacob's door more than a few times to ensure he didn't wander out of his room at three or four in the morning. We were so tired that we feared we might not wake when he woke. The kids' needs were so great. Sometimes, we look back and wonder how we made it through. I doubt we would have if not for our faith and God's goodness.

One of the most challenging parts was the pain of missing out on "normal parenting stuff." Our lives were filled with therapy appointments, horrendous meltdowns, exhaustion, and isolation. We longed just to plan play dates, enjoy family outings, play with our kids, and more.

Our love for Hannah and Jacob gave us the strength to continue, which has not changed. God was ever present, supplying what we needed day-to-day. Life was not what we had planned or expected, but it was still good.

The stress and at-home demands began to take a significant toll on Becky's health. She was having major health problems, including joint pain and circulation issues, resulting in

The Diagnoses

ulcerations on her feet and hands and profound fatigue. Once again, we struggled to get a diagnosis and to find the right medical professionals to help. Becky discovered an enlarged lymph node on her neck when Jacob was a baby in 1998. She showed it to doctors repeatedly throughout the years but could never get anyone to take it seriously or even do a biopsy. Being a pediatric oncology nurse, she knew this was something to be concerned about. Finally, in May of 2002, she saw a surgeon who, almost reluctantly, decided to perform a biopsy. He said he believed there was only a one in 500 chance it was lymphoma or leukemia. After the surgery, when the surgeon came to check on Becky, he said, "I tell you what, the damn thing looked scary!"

Two weeks later, we got a call to come into the office. On May 23, 2002, we heard the words no one wants to hear. They diagnosed Becky with a rare, chronic, non-curable, slow-growing form of non-Hodgkin's lymphoma. It was Memorial Weekend, and we had plans to go to the Black Hills for a camping trip. Becky asked the doctor if we should cancel our plans. He said, "No! Go raise hell!" After this conversation, we sat in silence for a few minutes. Jon repeatedly said to himself, *So, this is what it feels like!* We watch movies and hear stories about people receiving news of loved ones getting a diagnosis. Now, we could not believe it was happening to us. Becky broke the silence and said, "If I'm going to sit around and feel sorry for myself, I might as well already be dead!"

The next several months involved more biopsies, lab work, procedures, and meetings with health professionals. She was officially diagnosed with Waldenstrom Macroglobulinemia (WM), an exceedingly rare form of blood cancer.

We started calling ourselves the less than 5% family. We were two-for-two with children with Autism and now an extremely rare form of cancer. On top of all that, Becky's health was continuing to decline, with worsening symptoms, to the point that a vascular surgeon was contemplating amputating part of her foot because of an ulceration on her toe that would not heal due to poor circulation. Because WM is so rare, there was no specific treatment at that time. One oncologist told Becky this disease had an average life expectancy of five to eight years. Our kids were five and three years old at the time. Becky remembers thinking, *I know all kids need their mamas, but our kids really do!* It was a scary time.

Since then, Becky has received intermittent treatments and infusions through the years to keep her cancer in check. She has also been diagnosed with multiple autoimmune diseases, including Rheumatoid Arthritis, small vessel vasculitis, and Sjogren's Syndrome. All this, combined with the kids' growing needs, was intense, to say the least.

Once again, our God was faithful in so many ways and often in very tangible ways. A woman from our church in South Dakota showed up at our front door one day and said, "God told me to do your laundry." We did not hesitate to accept her help. For months, she picked up our dirty laundry twice weekly and returned it the next day neatly folded. What a tremendous help and source of encouragement.

In 2004, we sensed God calling us back into full-time ministry. This included a move back to Michigan. We were thankful to be in close proximity to family, with Jon's parents living only an hour away and his sister just two hours away. Their help and support were invaluable. After a few years in ministry, Jon returned to grad school to become a licensed professional counselor. This resulted in another career change. We are beyond thankful for all our amazing support here in Michigan from family, friends, and our church.

Friends have organized countless Meal Trains through the past 20 years. Some friends dropped off groceries. We remem-

The Diagnoses

ber one specific instance, a few years later, when our friend Emily surprised us with several gallons of apple juice and a 24-pack of toilet paper. These may seem like random items to deliver, but for us, it was perfect. Our Jacob used to drink apple juice by the gallon, and we were constantly running out. He also used a ridiculous amount of toilet paper, which often resulted in clogged toilets. This was a perfect grocery delivery for us and blessed us because it showed how well Emily knew us and what was happening in our home.

We were drowning in the day-to-day life of raising two children with Autism. We were adjusting to our new normal, which included the worlds of Autism and Cancer. We needed to refocus, readjust, and reframe our thinking. This is where God really began to reshape our story.

FOUR

Holland

Welcome to Holland
by Emily Perl Kingsley[1]
Reprinted by permission of the author

I am often asked to describe the experience of raising a child with a disability - to try to help people who have not shared that unique experience to understand it, to imagine how it would feel. It's like this……

When you're going to have a baby, it's like planning a fabulous vacation trip - to Italy. You buy a bunch of guide books and make your wonderful plans. The Coliseum. The Michelangelo David. The gondolas in Venice. You may learn some handy phrases in Italian. It's all very exciting.

After months of eager anticipation, the day finally arrives. You pack your bags and off you go. Several hours later, the plane lands. The flight attendant comes in and says, "Welcome to Holland."

I HAVE AWESOME (AUTISM)

"Holland?!?" you say. "What do you mean Holland?? I signed up for Italy! I'm supposed to be in Italy. All my life I've dreamed of going to Italy."

But there's been a change in the flight plan. They've landed in Holland and there you must stay.

The important thing is that they haven't taken you to a horrible, disgusting, filthy place, full of pestilence, famine and disease. It's just a different place.

So you must go out and buy new guide books. And you must learn a whole new language. And you will meet a whole new group of people you would never have met.

It's just a different place. It's slower-paced than Italy, less flashy than Italy. But after you've been there for a while and you catch your breath, you look around.... and you begin to notice that Holland has windmills....and Holland has tulips. Holland even has Rembrandts.

But everyone you know is busy coming and going from Italy... and they're all bragging about what a wonderful time they had there. And for the rest of your life, you will say "Yes, that's where I was supposed to go. That's what I had planned."

And the pain of that will never, ever, ever, ever go away... because the loss of that dream is a very very significant loss.

But... if you spend your life mourning the fact that you didn't get to Italy, you may never be free to enjoy the very special, the very lovely things ... about Holland.

Holland

Becky's mom introduced us to this short story via a Dear Abby article shortly after Hannah was diagnosed with Autism. We have shared it with many parents, friends, caregivers, family, and more throughout the years. This story highlights the struggles and celebrations of our Autism journey beautifully and accurately.

The first point of emphasis is essential—unmet and readjusted expectations in life. This is not the life we dreamed of, yet it is beautiful. And if we choose to find its joy and beauty, we can enjoy our new life here "in Holland." But that involves working through some very real and significant grief.

Most people think of grief as it relates to death, but our grief is the loss of many and ongoing dreams. It was and is important for us to sit in our grief and process it. If we do not work through our grief, how can we fully heal and find joy in what lies ahead? We have made it our goal to embrace and celebrate this new life, not just tolerate and survive it—but this was and continues to be a daily choice. The pain is ever-present. We are no longer simply "Mommy" and "Daddy" but have been thrust into roles we did not choose, such as social worker, speech therapist, advocate, researcher, educator, behaviorist, benefits coordinator, and more. We have become way too familiar with our local Social Security and DHHS offices.

We missed many events and activities with our kids through the years, including award ceremonies, sporting events, first dates, college decisions, and more. As we write this, our kids are young adults. At this stage of life, we thought we would be celebrating their college graduations, weddings, and maybe even grandchildren. The dream of grandparenting is all but lost for us.

We still have much to celebrate with our kids. Their celebrations are just very different. We celebrated the first and only birthday party invitation Jacob received from a peer, his friend

Katey, in elementary school. We also celebrated when Jacob learned to write his first and last name at the age of 23 and when he first made it through a church service without a meltdown. We were so proud when Hannah received the "Caring Friend Award" in 6th grade. Small victories become significant victories through the correct lens. Life in Holland is different than in Italy. Not less, just different. It is not the anticipated trip, but it is still a great destination.

We celebrate Hannah. She is very capable, strong-willed, social, and outgoing. She loves working with children, works a part-time job, has created her own successful small business, and has become a voice for the Autism community. She has embraced her Autism, including accepting opportunities to speak and share her story. She is a passionate advocate for those with disabilities. Even as a young child, she was very confident and secure. She saw her ability rather than her disability. At the age of five, she introduced herself to someone and said, "I have awesome!" referring to her autism. We reflect on this often and are so thankful she has fully embraced who God created her to be. As it says in the Bible, she is fearfully and wonderfully made (Psalm 139:14).

We celebrate Jacob. He is sweet, kind, sensitive, social, content, exceedingly schedule-oriented, and loves the little things in life, as evidenced by the fact that he is currently swinging in the hammock outside our camper. He captures the hearts of everyone he meets. Developmentally and emotionally, he functions at a five-to-six-year-old level. He is always up for a party if it is at our house. Yet, shortly after friends and family arrive, he makes his way to his room to decompress from all the stimulation. He will always be dependent on us or someone else for care in all areas of his life. We are "Forever Parents."

"Forever Parents!" We face ongoing stress and worry about our kids' future, specifically after we are unable to care for them. As Becky often says, "These are the thoughts and worries that keep me up at night." Jon feels the pressure to outlive our kids. This is especially true because of the uncertainty of Becky's chronic health issues and needs. Who will be there to care for them when we are gone? For special needs parents, this is an ongoing concern. Most parents would not choose to outlive their kids, but this is the case in our situation. We pray they have long, happy lives, but just one day shorter than ours.

Trick or treating with Dad!

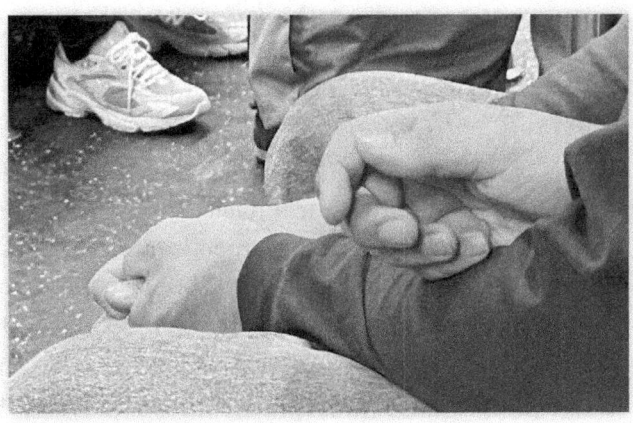

Dad is always near by...

Another reason we want to outlive our kids is because of their challenges in processing and understanding loss and separation. Hannah has the capacity to process grief and loss more effectively than her brother; although, it is still very difficult for her because she loves so big. She can find peace in the assurance that those she has lost are in Heaven with Jesus. For Jacob, the thought of Heaven is scary because he sees it as a forever separation. It brings him no comfort due to his lack of insight and understanding.

Jacob has anxiety anytime Jon is gone overnight. In the past, Jon traveled on occasion for work. Jacob would obsess over his return the entire time he was gone, even setting the timer for a countdown. Because of this, he slept with Dad's car keys for years. In his mind, this ensured Dad was home and not going anywhere. He still keeps track of the keys and can even be seen holding them in most pictures to this day, including his senior pictures. These concerns are significant and valid.

We find comfort in God's promises in Jeremiah 29:11, "'For I know the plans I have for you,' declares the Lord. 'Plans to prosper you, and not to harm you; to give you a hope and a future.'" God has a beautiful plan for our kids and their lives. He knows the challenges ahead, and God also knows what they will need all the days of their lives. He holds their futures in His hand! We can trust Him with their futures. We often remind ourselves of this and find hope in His promises.

Our kids love Jesus with all their hearts and love others as well. This is all that really matters. Our journey has taught us this, and we are thankful to have learned it from our children. This chapter has been difficult to write because we love our kids and do not want to give a negative impression of them or our lives. We would never want to change them, but the challenges are real. Both loving our life as it is and the grief of what could have been can coexist. We pray our story will provide others hope, encouragement, and validation on their journey.

FIVE

Building Blocks

We all need community, but on this journey, we need it even more. We have found it essential to build our village in multiple areas. Some of our most critical areas have been building our marriage, cultivating strong friendships, self-care, accessing community resources/networking, and our church family.

Build Your Marriage

We have often said we are a family rather than the label "parents of two kids with Autism." We need our marriage to not only survive but thrive, to provide the best family environment for all of us. One of the best ways to accomplish this is consistent date nights. In the Autism world, this can be extremely challenging because to enjoy a date night, you must first find a caregiver. Jacob is 25 years old, stands at a towering 6'5", and still needs a babysitter when we are away, and one that is fully trained because he also has epilepsy.

Weekend getaways are a real treat and much-needed—a

great time to reset, reconnect, and maybe even get a little rest. When our kids were younger, both sets of grandparents helped watch the kids to provide us life-giving breaks. Aunt Amy has been very supportive and helpful through the years. She took Hannah on her first girls' weekend to Chicago when Hannah was just 10 years old. They visited the American Girl Store, where Hannah got her first American Girl doll. She had been saving up to buy it for months. She still has that doll and the memories from their weekend together. This was just one of several weekend getaways with Aunt Amy. At the time of writing this, the two of them are flying out east next week with visits planned to New York City, DC, Long Island, and Pennsylvania. Hannah also has a strong peer group and has taken multiple trips with friends through the years. This support from our friends and family was and continues to be life-giving to our marriage.

We are very blessed with respite hours provided by the State of Michigan. But we know not everyone has access to this benefit. Even so, the struggle to find qualified caregivers is legitimate. It is easy to lose your marital identity amidst all the chaos. Work hard to make your marriage the best it can be.

Building Blocks

We know some of our friends on this journey are single parents. And for them, the challenges are magnified. We need to be mindful of this and step up whenever possible. This might mean something as simple as a text, a phone call, a mom/dad's night out, stepping in as a caregiver, and more.

Build Your Friendships

Surround yourself and your family with people who will celebrate your kids. This may be easier said than done. It takes time and energy to build strong relationships, and unfortunately, a lot of Autism parents have neither. Be mindful of those who take a special interest in your children and who your children respond to. Most likely, these are people more apt to "get it." Feeling the need to explain about our kids, their behaviors, their needs, and their quirks over and over is exhausting. Look for people who are compassionate and non-judgmental. For some, this is your family. However, this may not be the case for others, and you will need to seek out these supportive relationships elsewhere.

We will never forget the day of Jacob's graduation open

house. He was so excited for all his friends to come over. He had been talking about it for weeks. We explained the schedule for the day: first pizza, then say hi to your friends. So, that is what he did. He ate two slices of pizza, promptly walked out on the deck, and proudly exclaimed, "Hi friends!" Then, he went back to his room. He emerged a few minutes later in his jammies on the hunt for more pizza. Becky quickly asked him to change and explained that he could not wear his pajamas to his open house party. Jon immediately interjected, "Anyone who is not okay with Jacob in his jammies was not invited to his party." As we looked around, we realized he was right. We all need these types of friendships: those who are okay with us in jammies at our party.

We have also put effort into assisting our kids in building healthy friendships. This can be done by observing your child's peers, noting the kind and caring children, or asking their teachers for suggestions of who might be good buddies for your child. At one of Hannah's birthday parties, Becky's friend, Sunny, commented, "Hannah has such a nice group of friends." Becky responded, "Yep! I know, I chose them!" Of course, this is not entirely true. Our kids choose their own friends, but we definitely guided Hannah toward the girls we knew would be caring and accepting.

We were so blessed this past Christmas when Jacob's friends, Quentin and David, each gave him a sweet Christmas present. It has taken many years and assistance from his caregiver, Todd, to grow these friendships.

Building Blocks

Jacob and his buddy, Quentin

This was the first Christmas gift he received from a peer since first grade when his friend, Abby, gifted him a bag of rocks. That may sound like an odd Christmas gift, but it was perfect for our Jacob. Abby was a wonderful friend. She noticed Jacob dropping rocks through the drain on the playground. He loved watching and listening to them splash. So, Abby collected rocks from home, put them in a Christmas gift bag with a beautiful note, and gave them to Jacob. How beautiful is this? There were many tears of joy at our house that day. Someone saw our Jacob and valued him enough to take the time to collect rocks and bring them to school for him.

Just last year, Becky ran into Amy, Abby's mom, at a store. They started talking about our kids and reminiscing about this story. It still brings so much joy to both of them. Amy shared that Abby wrote a beautiful scholarship essay about this experience. Twenty years later, her act of kindness continues to inspire others.

I HAVE AWESOME (AUTISM)

Build in Time for Self-care

Again, we know how difficult this can be logistically and financially. Seek out even the smallest opportunity for some "me time." A fitting example of this, for us, is grocery shopping. Jon actually enjoys grocery shopping. It is one of his only opportunities to get some alone time. He is a mental health worker by day and a husband and autism dad at home.

Do not forget to laugh. We have found such joy and release in learning to laugh with our kids at the silly things they say and do. It truly is the best medicine. We love sharing our Hannah and Jacob stories; our friends cannot wait to hear them. This helps them love our kids even more. Here are a few of our classics.

It had been a long day. We transferred Jon's dad from the hospital to a rehab facility after he re-fractured his hip. Jacob was beyond done for the day, and we headed to McDonald's. If you have a kid with Autism, you know we keep McDonald's in business. There is just something about our kids and McDonald's chicken and french fries. At this point in time, we were milliseconds from a meltdown, and the cashier informed us that there would be a wait for the fries. Not good! We managed for a few minutes, but Jacob raised his hand, ready to hit his dad. But, his arm froze, and Jacob said, "You hit me; I'll beat your ass!" In Jacob language, this meant he was about to lose it, and someone was going to get hit. Jon turned and looked at the cashier. Her eyes were as big as saucers. She frantically hollered, "Ah, how are we coming on the fries?" Oh, my goodness, we have laughed about that for years, and that poor young lady did not know what to do! But our laughter at the moment diffused a lot of anxiety.

Our sweet Hannah likes to use the Bible to keep us in line. When she was around six years old, Becky was talking with her about her attitude and explained she needed to apologize.

She stopped, thought about it, and confidently said, "Mommy, everybody sins every day. Remember yesterday when you were grumpy? That was sinning! Do you have something you want to say to Daddy?" How do you respond to that?

And finally, this is one of our all-time favorite Jacob stories. He was in elementary school. He came home from school and kept repeating the same phrase. We struggled, at first, to figure out what he was saying. Then, we realized he was saying, "Miss Shari is hot." Just for reference, Miss Shari was one of his beloved paraeducators. We looked at each other and burst into laughter. Over the next few weeks, we learned the backstory of this hilarious comment. They had popcorn at school one day, and as Jacob grabbed a handful, Miss Shari quickly reminded him that it was hot and this was what Jacob was referring to. So, Jacob was telling us that Miss Shari said the popcorn was hot, but it simply came out as "Miss Shari is hot!" The funniest part is that Jacob continues to repeat this whenever he sees her. You just cannot make this stuff up! As Jon says often, "We will never be bored!"

As part of self-care, remembering to give ourselves grace has also been important. We need to realize we cannot always be on top of our game. As our kids' preschool teacher, Karen, told us, "It's a marathon, not a sprint!"

We also make every effort to keep our lives simple versus stressful. This includes basic things like using paper plates to simplify clean-up, hiring a friend to clean our house monthly, and letting go of unrealistic expectations in many areas. And we happily utilize therapy as needed. We are always in search of life-giving things.

Build Resources and Network

Accessing resources takes an unbelievable amount of time, energy, and research. Again, this is not something Autism parents have in abundance. But once you have done the work, you can reap the benefits. Resources vary by community.

We are blessed with great resources in our community. Respite and Community Living Services (CLS) hours through Easter Seals MORC are at the top of our list. They have provided us with much-needed respite and empowered our kids to continue to grow and develop with the assistance of a one-on-one direct care staff. They work with our kids on goals we have formulated with our case manager to promote their continued growth. We have been blessed with many wonderful caregivers through the years.

Your local ARC office is a great place to look for resources. Ours in Oakland County, Michigan, has assisted us with everything from estate planning to accessing Medicaid to questions about available benefits.

We have also found it beneficial to find summer activities or day camps accommodating our kids. Our community provides a wonderful program called Clarkston Scamp. It is a five-week summer day camp in our community, providing fantastic opportunities for those with special needs. Scampers enjoy many activities throughout the summer, including bowling, movies, field trips, visiting our local county fair, Legoland, and weekly park days filled with swimming, fishing, boating, and more. Scamp is fully staffed, providing the support each scamper needs to help ensure a successful summer. One of the most beautiful features of Scamp is you never age out. So many supports end at the age of 26. Our Jacob loves Scamp and just completed his 20th year. Because we place such high value on Clarkston Scamp, we have become very active in fundraising, promoting, and supporting Scamp in any way we can, even serving on fundraiser committees. As parents, we must stay active in supporting these programs that support our kids to ensure they will remain available.

Sometimes, great support or opportunities are right in front

Building Blocks

of us, and we just don't know them yet. This is why keeping our eyes and ears open is essential. Becky and Hannah visited our local library a few years ago and noticed one of Hannah's former classmates putting away books and videos. Immediately, Becky thought this might be something for Hannah. She requested a meeting with the director, Julie.

Initially, Hannah began volunteering at the library with the help of her friend/job coach, Rachel. Within a couple of weeks, Hannah was able to work independently. Two months later, they offered her a paid position. Hannah has worked at the library in multiple capacities over the past five years. She has been very successful there and loves her job and the community it provides. The staff at the library was and continues to be incredibly accommodating and supportive.

I HAVE AWESOME (AUTISM)

This past fall, Becky and Hannah attended a conference offering a gratitude wall. This is what Hannah wrote and hung on that wall: "Thankful for a job that understands me!" What more can we ask for? We found this job by simply looking around our community and seeking opportunities for employment for Hannah.

During COVID, when Jacob was off school, we were desperate to find things for him and his caregiver to do. We

Building Blocks

are so blessed to have Clarkston Family Farm, just two miles from our house. Because our caregiver at the time, Rachel, was deemed an essential worker, she could take Jacob to the farm multiple days a week, even during the entire lockdown. There, they cared for the gardens, watered and fed the animals, collected eggs, and much more. He loved it and continues volunteering there four days a week with his current caregiver, Todd. It has been a lifesaver for the past four-plus years. It gives him a sense of purpose, community, pride, and, best of all, joy.

I HAVE AWESOME (AUTISM)

Building Blocks

In our community, those with special needs are valued and supported by many. One notable example of this is our local downtown diner, 2 South Brunch House. Through the years, we have become friends with the employees at 2 South. Sunday lunch there quickly became our weekly routine during COVID.

Jacob and Maria our server from 2 South Brunch House

Post-COVID, 2 South no longer offers carry-out services on Sundays. However, because they understand Jacob's challenges when waiting for a table and food after our morning at church, they happily provide carry-out for our family every Sunday. Maria, one of the servers, even lovingly writes Jacob's name on his to-go container, which is, of course, always the same thing—chicken tenders and fries for lunch.

Another fitting example of community support is our local mechanic. As previously mentioned, Jacob is obsessed with

Dad's keys and our cars. So, when we need to take a car into the shop, we have to work around his school schedule and ensure we have it back before he arrives home. Kora, the office manager/receptionist at Morgans Car Service, graciously understands our situation and realizes we need our car back home by 2:00 p.m. whenever possible. This may sound like something small but it is huge to our family. It has helped us avoid numerous meltdowns. We are beyond thankful for many in our community who continue to be supportive, as highlighted by the above examples. The lesson in this is to keep your eyes open and look for support and all the possible opportunities around you.

Hannah with Kora from Morgan's Service

Build Your Education Team

Building a dedicated team for your child takes a lot of effort and time. For us, it was critical to be in their schools and classrooms as much as possible. We strived to build strong relationships with all staff and faculty, including bus drivers, lunchroom staff, custodians, social workers, speech therapists, OT/PT, teachers, paraeducators, office staff, and principals. Building strong relationships will make it easier and more natural for the staff to connect with your child and family. Because, like it or not, this is a family affair. A unified team is a huge part of giving your child an optimal educational experience. We have been blessed with many wonderful education teams through the years.

We realize this is not everyone's experience. Sometimes, you may need to explore other avenues for your educational support. That is a personal decision for each family to make. It is important to remember, in all of this, that you know your child best. You are their best advocate. And, unfortunately, in some instances, you may be their only advocate. Advocacy is not a role we chose; it was chosen for us once we had a child with special needs. There is an art to advocacy—finding the balance between being assertive but not aggressive or passive. Trust your heart.

It is important to research your community and available school systems. When we moved to Michigan from South Dakota in 2004, we spent time meeting with area schools and special education directors. These meetings helped us determine where we wanted to purchase a home. Then, we met with our realtor.

Can we talk about IEPs (Individualized Education Plan)? Just the mention of it can raise anxiety. First, always bring snacks—homemade is even better. This is not bribery. It is just showing your team you value them. Secondly, it is unrealistic and unfair to think we can get everything on our wish list for our child. Sometimes, we need to invent our own alternatives and accommodations. For example, when Hannah was a senior in high school, she wanted to work in a preschool setting to gain work experience. This was not something that was available through the school at that time. Becky went into major network mode. She secured a volunteer position five mornings a week at an area church preschool. The lessons Hannah learned there were invaluable. This, of course, changed her school schedule, which meant Becky did some homeschooling with Hannah that semester. It was not an easy semester, but it was what Hannah needed at the time.

It seems our kids are always transitioning to a new program, building, and/or team. This can be stressful for our kids and us as parents. Plan often and early! Jacob is about to turn 26 years old. This means he will age out of our school's adult transition program. This year will be his last. We began planning for this transition almost a year ago. This involves looking for potential programs, supports, and services. Our education team has been helpful in assisting with this.

Build Your Faith Community

Our church community has become family. Unfortunately for many, finding a faith community that supports their special needs children has been a challenge—according to the blog Church4EveryChild, "Nearly 50% (46.6%) of special needs parents said they refrain from participating in religious activities because their child was not included or welcomed."The referenced article continues to summarize research: "Fatigue was a common parental characteristic cited as preventing inclusion of a child at church. Many parents indicated a strong desire for a church community but, as one put it, because of our child's needs 'we have not had the time or energy to seek-out and prepare (educate) a new spiritual home for ourselves. Therefore, we do not attend regular weekly services anywhere, as much as we could really use the support and spiritual community.'"[2]

Building Blocks

In our opinion, this research is sad and unacceptable. Church should be the first place our friends on the fringes are welcomed. When we read scripture, we find Jesus speaking about "the least of these" (Matthew 25:40). Our kids are part of this group—often forgotten and undervalued. But as we raise awareness and bring our kids into mainstream churches, we shine a light on the need.

We have helped launch special needs ministries at two different churches. It may sound daunting, but in our experience, these families simply seek a place to belong and grow in their faith. Our monthly events offer BINGO with prizes, music, dancing, and pizza for special needs individuals and their families/caregivers. This brings a whole new meaning to the line from the movie *Field of Dreams*, "If you build it, they will come!"[3]

Our church also provides one-on-one buddies to assist special needs kids in attending their age-appropriate classes with their peers. This helps ensure a successful Sunday morning experience for the whole family and allows parents the much-needed opportunity to attend the worship service. The key is finding a church that places enough value on our community to build it.

We are blessed to have found a supportive church community. Hannah volunteers weekly in the nursery with the babies. She is valued, not only by the church staff, but by the parents as well. Several young moms communicate with Hannah throughout the week, often expressing appreciation for all she does for their kids. They also send photos they know she will enjoy. A couple of moms have even texted her to let her know their child was asking for her. This has provided another village of support that is hers alone. This has nothing to do with Mom and Dad; this is all hers. Hannah has independently joined multiple small group Bible studies. Several have commented on her depth of understanding of the Bible and its overall message. She is an active contributing part of these groups. THEY SEE HER.

Jacob absolutely loves attending our worship services each week. He will re-watch them on YouTube over and over throughout the following week. Every Sunday, multiple people come out of their way to greet him and are thrilled if he responds. Many have shared with us how blessed they are by his worship each Sunday. He stands and twists through all the songs. His Autism superpower is his amazing memory, so he quickly learns the words to the songs. Often, he will begin singing along spontaneously. We cannot explain how this touches our hearts. We are sure our LORD is smiling as Jacob brings his sacrifice of praise. This speaks to the beauty of this community. What we feared some would consider a distraction and annoyance has blessed so many.

Building Blocks

Jon and Jacob were able to attend "Man Camp" (Men's Retreat) this past year. All the men were so welcoming and accepting of him. Jacob cannot wait to go back again this year.

I HAVE AWESOME (AUTISM)

Becky's friend, Margaret, was asked by a friend why she chose to come to our church. She explained that they want to be part of a faith community that values all people, and a perfect example is how our Jacob is valued. Each Sunday morning, a group meets before service. We form a circle, share upcoming events and highlights, and pray together. During this time, our Jacob almost always spins around in the middle of the circle. No one seems bothered or annoyed. But even more than that, they celebrate it and who God created him to be. As Margaret said, "This is why we are at this church. Jacob is 'helicoptering around' in the middle of the circle, and no one even blinks an eye." THEY SEE HIM.

SIX

Finding Their Niche

Assisting our children in finding their niche has been of utmost importance to us. We started by considering their strengths and, more importantly, their areas of interest. Do not be surprised if you find these in the most unlikely places.

Hannah worked at our local library, but only four to five hours per week. Becky began researching, networking, and looking for a productive way for Hannah to spend some of her free time. Plus, Mama needed a break. Hannah's therapist, who we all love, recommended a creative outlet to help lessen her anxiety.

We visited The Art Experience in Pontiac and immediately knew this was the place for her. Hannah had no interest in any art classes in school, but this seemed different. The Art Experience is staffed with certified art therapists. Hannah began attending open sessions 2-3 times a week. Her time there helped lessen her anxiety and build her confidence as she began creating beautiful, one-of-a-kind pieces. She started posting some of her creations, and soon, people began placing custom orders. In November 2019, we hosted a customer appreciation open house to highlight Hannah's work. It was a tremendous success, and she nearly sold out of everything. From there, we started doing craft shows, and she became a vendor at a local shop, Yellow Dog Marketplace, in Clarkston. This is how her business, Hannah Joy Spectrum Designs, was born.

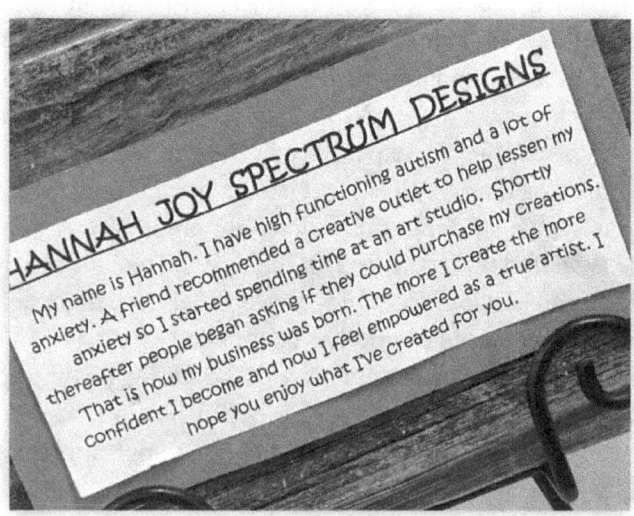

HANNAH JOY SPECTRUM DESIGNS

My name is Hannah. I have high functioning autism and a lot of anxiety. A friend recommended a creative outlet to help lessen my anxiety so I started spending time at an art studio. Shortly thereafter people began asking if they could purchase my creations. That is how my business was born. The more I create the more confident I become and now I feel empowered as a true artist. I hope you enjoy what I've created for you.

Finding Their Niche

Hannah's business continues to grow. She was featured on ClickonDetroit for World Autism Day in April of 2021. She now sells her items in stores nationwide, including venues in Michigan, Long Island, Boston, Estes Park, North Carolina, & South Carolina. We also sell at many craft and vendor shows throughout the year. We even purchased a travel trailer to take

I HAVE AWESOME (AUTISM)

her business mobile as a family affair. It has indeed been a joy for all of us. Hannah enjoys meeting new customers and sharing her story. She has even spoken at a couple of events sharing about the birth of her business. She is a fierce advocate and loves being a "voice for her people," in her words.

This past year has provided Hannah with yet another opportunity to promote her business and raise awareness about the many abilities of those who are neurodivergent. Our friend, Amy, founded Urban Vine, an organization that provides employment and entrepreneurial opportunities for adults with special needs. They create all-natural products and hand-made gift items.

Urban Vine has partnered with USA Today Bestselling author Viola Shipman (Wade Rouse) to offer gift baskets complementing several of his novels. They have now asked Hannah and some other entrepreneurs with special needs to contribute some of their handmade items to their gift baskets. Hannah even appeared on their weekly social media vidcast to share her business.

We love watching her shine as she inspires others. Never in our wildest dreams did we envision her with a thriving craft business. So, keep an open mind when exploring options for your kids.

Finding Their Niche

Visiting "One for All", Hannah is an artisan at this shop in Long Island, NY

Hannah sharing her story at an Oakland County Health Network meeting

Hannah at an event with Amy Vine and Wade Rouse

I HAVE AWESOME (AUTISM)

Becky grew up on a farm in Central Iowa. Her family raised pigs and grew corn and soybeans on 240 acres. It was a family farm, previously farmed by her grandfather. When her family moved to the farm, Grandpa Faust came multiple times a week to help her dad learn the ropes.

Jon grew up on a 10-acre hobby farm in Grand Ledge, Michigan. His dad tapped maple trees to make syrup. Later in his life, he purchased a small cider press and began making apple cider using apples from their orchard. He also raised chickens. We enjoyed many breakfasts at Grandpa and Grandma's house through the years, featuring his homemade sourdough pancakes with fresh maple syrup and delicious apple cider.

Finding Their Niche

Our rich family history makes it unsurprising that Jacob enjoys his time at Clarkston Family Farm. It is complete with sweet corn and pigs, just like Becky's family farm in Iowa, as well as apple cider and fresh maple syrup reminiscent of time spent at the acreage where Jon grew up in Michigan. It was a logical place for him to land.

Hannah's original desire was to work in childcare. She tried caregiving in multiple settings, including working with special needs adults. None of these were a fit. Now, she owns and operates a thriving small business. We never saw that one coming. On the other hand, Jacob has always loved the outdoors, farm animals, and the simple things in life. His love for Clarkston Family Farm is a natural fit.

It is important to keep an open mind, embrace your child's uniqueness, search for hidden talents, and allow them to be experiential learners while in pursuit of his/her dreams. As parents, we desire to encourage our children to seek new experiences and to reach their full potential. It is often difficult to find the balance between encouraging and pushing them to explore new directions while keeping in mind their true limitations related to their disabilities. This is especially true with Hannah because she is so high functioning and has an extraordinarily strong skill set. In times of increased stress and anxiety, it is easy to forget that she has autism and processing difficulties. We strive to step back and provide the support she needs during these times. There is no exact science behind this process. One day at a time.

SEVEN

Lessons Learned and Still Learning

Part of allowing our kids to grow and develop comes through new experiences, even when scary and intimidating. If we do not stretch our kids, they will never adapt and grow, and we will be home with them endlessly. There were years when we could not go out to eat without fear of complete meltdowns in public. So, we stayed home. As a couple, we finally decided to make eating out a point of emphasis. Jon often said, "We need to get over ourselves. Who cares what kind of looks and judgment we get." It was a tough road, but now we can enjoy meals out as a family. It was worth the effort and the risk of public humiliation. This same principle can apply in many different areas.

I HAVE AWESOME (AUTISM)

Our family loves traveling and camping. When we travel, we are often out in public, near other travelers. It was hard when the kids were younger because Jacob was an early riser and had no idea how to use a quiet voice so others could sleep. Not all fellow campers were gracious and understanding. Jon often drove him around, sightseeing for a couple of hours in the early mornings until around 8 a.m., when we knew others were beginning to wake. This was not always fun but has paid significant dividends, and now we travel and enjoy camping all over the country. Of course, we still have our challenges, but we are all learning and growing.

Lessons Learned and Still Learning

When we travel, we also adjust our sightseeing schedules to allow Jacob a day of rest between all-day excursions. He needs this to decompress and rest. Our outings are much more successful when we accommodate his needs while still pushing and encouraging him to participate in new things. We would often love a big family hike or one last drive through a national park, but we are restricted because of Jacob's needs. Obviously, we understand this, but it is still frustrating. We remind each other we are a family, and we all need to make sacrifices sometimes for each other. This is what families do. In return, Jacob has taught us to slow down on vacation. This is one of the many valuable lessons from our kids.

We have learned through the years that meeting some of our kids' basic needs will ensure a more successful and enjoyable trip for everyone. When we camp, we scout and find sites with great hammocking trees. Jacob spends hours a day in his hammock, which is therapeutic for his sensory system. We also need a campground that offers Wi-Fi. He loves listening to worship music and watching his favorite movies, including *The Parent Trap, Father of the Bride 2, The Pacifier, College Road Trip, Home Alone*, and *Veggie Tales*. This is very calming for him. Jon and Becky also love Wi-Fi to enjoy a movie and a glass of wine at the end of a long day. On our most recent trip, we paid an extra $120 for a hotspot to ensure Wi-Fi access. It was definitely money well spent.

I HAVE AWESOME (AUTISM)

Even when we plan and try to make all the accommodations, life can be very unpredictable. That is one of the most challenging parts. We do not always know what might trigger a meltdown.

We had a crazy experience at Glacier National Park two years ago. The fog was thick, and we had just crossed Logan Pass on Going to the Sun Road. Jacob was completely done, but we were at least two hours from our campground. We tried everything to calm him but had no luck. He became so frustrated and overwhelmed that he started hitting Jon while he was trying to drive in the thick fog on the winding mountain roads. Feeling the need to return as quickly as possible, we did not realize we exceeded the 25-mph speed limit. A friendly park ranger did notice, however, and pulled us over. Jacob was not happy we stopped, and as the ranger approached our truck, he hit Jon again. Becky was in tears trying to explain our situation. The ranger was gracious and did not issue a ticket. He said, "I know you have a lot going on here, but if you do not slow down, you will hit someone and have a whole different situation." That was stressful, but we would not trade our trip to Glacier for anything. Despite this, Jacob keeps asking to go back. So many lessons were learned on that trip.

Lessons Learned and Still Learning

Holidays are also big triggers. Becky loves hosting and has always dreamed of big family Christmas parties. For all families, the holidays tend to come with unrealistic expectations. It is no different for our family. Because of this, we have created new family traditions that make for a more enjoyable and less stressful holiday situation for everyone. These are not what we initially hoped for, but we have grown to love and appreciate our modified, less busy Christmas seasons. It leaves more time for reflection on the true meaning of Christmas.

Our family attends the church service on Christmas Eve each year, followed by carry-out pizza. We then have a little birthday party for Jesus, complete with a cake that is a great teaching tool about the birth of Jesus. Then, we open our gifts under the tree. Once the kids are in bed, Santa fills the stockings and brings more presents. Our Jacob is always so excited about Santa. He starts counting down the days to Christmas Eve each year mid-summer. After we take inventory of our gifts from Santa, we head to the local movie theater for a throwback mid-morning Christmas movie in our jammies. The rest of Christmas Day is spent at home enjoying basketball and football games with many delicious snacks. Jacob always requests ham and baked potatoes for Christmas dinner.

After Christmas, as schedules allow, we try to get together for small family gatherings. This has worked beautifully for us. We need to permit ourselves not to attend events and family gatherings that we know will trigger our kids and not feel guilty about it.

Lessons Learned and Still Learning

Attending sporting events has also been challenging. Our family loves sports and attending games. We live in Metro Detroit and have access to multiple venues. When our kids were young, attending events was nearly impossible for them. The environment was too overstimulating and loud, requiring too much time sitting in their seats. For several years, we were

I HAVE AWESOME (AUTISM)

blessed with complimentary tickets to Detroit Tigers games for their Annual Autism Recognition Days. The organization Jack's Place for Autism provided these tickets, and many special needs families spread out throughout the stadium for these games. A couple of the years, Hannah was privileged to meet some of the players and their wives before the game. One year, she even helped throw out the first pitch.

Because the tickets were complimentary, we could leave early if that was what our kids needed. In the first year, we only made it to the third inning, followed by the fifth inning, and the seventh inning of our third year. And in our fourth year, we

Lessons Learned and Still Learning

enjoyed a walk-off home run in the bottom of the ninth inning. This was a massive accomplishment for our whole family. We were more excited about this than we were about the home run.

Just last year, our whole family attended a Michigan State University football game. We prepared ourselves with realistic expectations that we might not make it through the entire game. We knew Jacob would struggle to understand the break at half time. We were concerned he would think the game was over and it was time to go home, so we told him we were going to two football games. This worked like a charm, and he not only stayed for the entire game but also really seemed to enjoy it. He keeps asking us to go to another game. These examples highlight why it is so important to stretch our kids, even if it puts us in uncomfortable situations.

It is also essential to accept the things we cannot do or change for now, remembering that this may not last forever. Our kids have grown so much in the last 20 years. We have enjoyed things with them that we would have never dreamed possible.

EIGHT

Grace Upon Grace

This is a challenging journey. We need to be grace givers, especially to ourselves. As we shared previously, Hannah was diagnosed just before her third birthday. Once we found out about her Autism, we had many regrets and guilt surrounding the way we had parented and disciplined her. Our girl has always been strong-willed, oppositional, independent, and a free spirit. She definitely lives up to the red hair hype. Over the years, we have apologized to Hannah for our parenting missteps. She has been gracious and forgiven us.

As parents, we also need to forgive ourselves for the things we did not know—for the times we lost it with our kids and for the times we failed to manage our anger. And to be honest, we need to offer ourselves forgiveness for the times we have chosen self-pity and have looked around at others and thought about how life would be so much easier without Autism. It is hard to admit this because we do not want it to be misconstrued and imply that we do not love our kids just as they are. But Autism is hard, and that is a fact. We hope to find joy amidst the difficulty.

Our Jacob tries our patience often. He obsessively, and

we mean *obsessively*, asks Becky the same questions repeatedly. And no one can answer him except Mom. In his mind, it must be her. At times, when we have become frustrated, we stop and reflect on how awful it must be for him to have that much anxiety all the time. This perspective gives us what we need to continue with a measure of patience, most of the time.

Jacob's CLS worker, Todd, had a brilliant idea. We made a social story with tokens, explaining he can only ask Mom three daily questions. His wonderful teacher, Michelle, made a cute token board which hangs on our refrigerator. When he sees Mom, he makes a beeline for the fridge and grabs it. We even take it with us when we go camping and on vacations. It has been a game-changer.

Grace Upon Grace

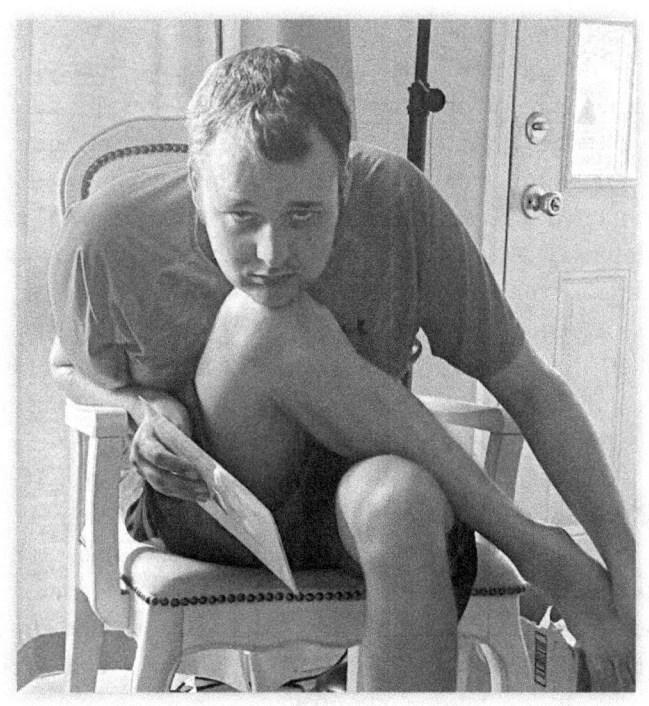

I HAVE AWESOME (AUTISM)

As we explained previously, our kids are on opposite ends of the spectrum. Their struggles are vastly different. Both struggle with impulse control and anxiety, but it manifests with different symptoms. Jacob's anxiety and frustration are expressed through physical outbursts. This has improved as he has matured, but we still have holes in our walls to prove it. His intensity during these times can be explosive. Many times, we do not even know what triggered the behavior. For us, the key is to remain calm and avoid raising our voices. He hates it when he feels like he is in trouble or when someone is upset with him. Our job is to keep the temperature down during these times, and it's not always easy.

Hannah's anxiety and frustration are expressed verbally. Once again, it is important to keep the temperature down. We have learned, and are still learning, that the best time to share constructive criticism is not in the middle of the meltdown. We need to wait until she is in a teachable place. Jon has often said, "Nobody ever wins an argument." Much of Hannah's recent frustration comes because her life is approaching a transition point. She still wants to live at home but longs for independence and does not enjoy many parenting tips. It is a tricky spot for her and us. It is easy to forget she has Autism because she is so high-functioning. We need to remind ourselves that she struggles with processing and anxiety, too . We need to be mindful about giving her grace.

For now, both kids living at home works best for our family. We recently remodeled our basement and created a little apartment for Hannah. She loves her new space. It provides her with a place that is all her own. Hannah and Jacob are remarkably close, literally best friends. They would be devastated if not together. And we love being a family of four. Most of the time.

Grace Upon Grace

Offering grace to others can be difficult. We need to remember that most people do not understand our journey, and, to be honest, this is an unrealistic expectation. What we do hope is that others will choose to learn as much as they can and thus be more supportive. We also need to offer forgiveness and understanding to people when they say the wrong things that are hurtful and invalidating.

Our hope is others will join us on this journey. They do not need all the answers, just a kind and compassionate heart. The Bible speaks to this in Romans 12:15, "Rejoice with those who rejoice; mourn with those who mourn." Mourning with those who mourn does not mean offering pity. Instead, it means coming alongside with support, understanding, and validation, and rejoicing with others should come naturally.

The things we rejoice over are different from most families. We do not have school award nights, MVP awards, college scholarships, engagement parties, or gender reveals. We are happy to celebrate these special times with others, but in return hope others will celebrate our children's achievements, even if it is something as simple as being highlighted as "Volunteer of the Month" at Clarkston Family Farm. We are called to share each other's burdens and joys. Just as Jesus carries our burdens, we are called to carry each other's and also celebrate together. Oh, if we could all just learn to live like this, what a different place this world would be.

Grace Upon Grace

We will highlight a few final points as we reflect on our story. Prayer. We pray often. We pray over our parenting decisions. We ask others to pray with us for wisdom, patience, and strength. We believe in the power of prayer and that our God loves to hear from us. He wants to carry our burdens and worries. We can run to Him, always.

Also, trust your heart. You know your kids better than anyone. You know what they need. Block out critical outside voices. Trust your instincts and intuition. Seek information and wise counsel, but in the end, trust your heart. And remember, God has given us our children. He has equipped us with all we need in our parenting journey. He loves our kids and us more than we could ever imagine. We pray you find joy on the journey, even on the most challenging days. WE SEE YOU!

Epilogue

Mom and Dad,

I have dreamt of being a voice for my people (the Autism community), and you have helped make this possible by writing this book. Thank you, Mom and Dad, for doing so much for my brother, Jacob and me. We're so blessed to have such wonderful parents who advocate and fight for our needs.

Thank you, Mom and Dad, for your unconditional love and patience through the good and challenging times. Thank you, Dad, for tirelessly working hard to provide for us. Thank you for the many walks and times spent together. Thank you, Mom, for being an endless advocate for Jacob and me and for the long days helping me with Hannah Joy Spectrum Designs.

You have helped Jacob and me to see the value of having autism, and you have embraced it as well. Because of this, other families admire you both, not only for how you accept our autism but also for enjoying it. I thank God for blessing me with wonderful parents and a brother who makes me laugh daily. I love you both and wish every other child could have parents like you.

Love, Hannah

Acknowledgements

This book has been a dream of ours for years —but life. Thank you to those who persisted in encouraging us to share our story; believing that our story will support and encourage others on a similar journey.

Thank you to the United House Publishing team for helping these rookies navigate the publishing process. Thank you for valuing our story and assisting us in bringing it to life.

Notes

1. Kingsley, Emily Perl. "Welcome to Holland." Emily Perl Kingsley, 2024, https://www.emilyperlkingsley.com/welcome-to-holland.

2. Grcevich, Dr. Stephen. "What are the stats on disability and church?" Church4EveryChild. February 9. 2016, https://church4everychild.org/2016/02/09/what-are-the-stats-on-disability-and-church/#:~:text=Nearly%2050%25%20(46.6%25)%20of,was%20not%20included%20or%20welcomed.

3. Robinson, Phil Alden, dir. Field of Dreams. Universal City, CA: Universal Pictures, 1989.

About the Author

Jon and Becky Richey have been married for 32 years. They live in Metro Detroit with their two Autistic young adult children. They enjoy traveling, camping, and exploring as a family. Jon is always up for a hike, kayaking or anything outdoors. He works as a mental health professional at a local junior high school. Becky loves capturing pictures on their excursions. She spends much of her time assisting their daughter, Hannah with her booming craft business and ensuring their son, Jacob has access to local services and opportunities. Socialization and independence have always been primary goals for their children. Their life is full, crazy and never boring.